COMMUNITY · CONNECTIONS

?

GETTING TO KNOW OUR PLANET
SOUTH AMERICAN CLOUD FOREST

BY VICKY FRANCHINO

CHERRY LAKE Publishing

Published in the United States of America by Cherry Lake Publishing
Ann Arbor, Michigan
www.cherrylakepublishing.com

Content Adviser: Linda Hooper-Bùi, PhD, Associate Professor, Department of
Environmental Science, Louisiana State University Agricultural Center, Baton Rouge, Louisiana
Reading Adviser: Marla Conn, Read With Me Now

Photo Credits: Cover and page 1, © Glenn R. Specht-grs photo/Shutterstock.com; page 5,
© Elliotte Rusty Harold/Shutterstock.com; pages 7, 9, and 13, © Dr. Morley Read/
Shutterstock.com; page 11, © rebvt/Shutterstock.com; page 15, © Lighttraveler/Shutterstock.com;
page 17, © Phoo Chan/Shutterstock.com; page 19, © 3523studio/Shutterstock.com; page 21,
© KalypsoWorldPhotography/Shutterstock.com.

LIBRARY OF CONGRESS CATALOGING-IN-PUBLICATION DATA
Names: Franchino, Vicky, author.
  Title: South American cloud forest / by Vicky Franchino.
Description: Ann Arbor, Michigan : Cherry Lake Publishing, [2016] |
  Series: Community connections | Series: Getting to know our planet | Audience:
  K to grade 3. | Includes bibliographical references and index.
Identifiers: LCCN 2015039839| ISBN 9781634705196 (lib. bdg.) |
  ISBN 9781634706391 (pbk.) | ISBN 9781634705790 (pdf) |
  ISBN 9781634706995 (ebook)
Subjects: LCSH: Cloud forests—South America—Juvenile literature. |
  Cloud forest ecology—Juvenile literature.
Classification: LCC QH541.5.C63 F73 2016 | DDC 577.34—dc23
  LC record available at http://lccn.loc.gov/2015039839

Cherry Lake Publishing would like to acknowledge the
work of The Partnership for 21st Century Skills. Please
visit www.p21.org for more information.

Printed in the United States of America
Corporate Graphics
January 2016

SOUTH AMERICAN CLOUD FOREST

CONTENTS

MOUNTAINTOP FOREST

Imagine you're a bird. You fly up into the Andes Mountains of South America. Soon, heavy fog and a **canopy** of trees surround you. Welcome to the cloud forest! This **biome** is found in very high places. It is usually 5,000 to 10,000 feet (1,524 to 3,048 meters) above sea level.

Cloud forests are named for the clouds of mist that often fill the area.

The cloud forest is filled with amazing animals and plants. Scientists are working hard to learn more about the forest. What do you know about the cloud forest? What do you still wonder about it?

5

Cloud forests are found in the tropics. The tropics lie just north and south of the **equator**. This is an imaginary line circling the middle of Earth. The weather is usually warm and moist in the tropics. The temperature doesn't change much from summer to winter.

Many plants thrive in the warm, wet, tropical cloud forest.

Dead plant matter carries important **nutrients**. These nutrients enter the soil when the plants break down. But they need sunlight to break down. Fog blocks much of the sunlight in cloud forests. Can you guess how this affects the soil?

7

DRINKING THE FOG

Plants in the cloud forest are often dripping wet. Has it just rained? The answer is probably no. A lot of the forest's water comes from the clouds. The trees don't just soak up water through their roots. They "drink" it through their leaves! They also get important nutrients from this cloud water.

Wide leaves soak in water from the air around them.

LOOK!

Cloud forest plants
need a lot of
moisture. Watch the
weather around you.
Is there a lot of rain
or fog where you
live? Could cloud
forest plants live near
your home?

Other plants also rely on the clouds for water. Moss and lichen act like sponges. They soak up moisture from the air. **Epiphytes** grow on top of other plants. They don't get their food from these plants. They get it from the air and the clouds. Epiphytes are also known as air plants. They don't need soil to grow!

Epiphytes do not hurt the plants they grow on.

THINK!

Plants aren't the only things that rely on cloud water. People do, too! In some parts of the forest, about half of the fresh water comes from the clouds. What would happen if we lost this source of water? What would people, plants, and animals do?

11

CREATURES OF THE CLOUD FOREST

The cloud forest is among the world's most **diverse** areas. Many kinds of living things are found there. Scientists are still discovering new ones! One recent discovery was the olinguito. This animal is related to raccoons. Some people think it looks a bit like a teddy bear! Scientists have also found new kinds of wood lizards. They look like miniature dragons!

In 2006, experts only knew about six types of wood lizard. Now they know about 15 of them!

Shouldn't scientists have discovered all of Earth's animals by now? Think about all the living things in the world. Why do you think scientists are still finding new creatures in the cloud forest?

13

Some cloud forest animals might also live near your home. Squirrels and mice are two examples. Other cloud forest animals aren't found anywhere else. The spectacled bear lives mostly in South America. It gets its name from yellow markings around its eyes that look like glasses. "Spectacles" is another word for "eyeglasses." This bear is an **omnivore**. It eats both plants and animals.

The spectacled bear is the only bear in South America.

Sometimes, plants and animals help each other survive. Many animals rely on the cloud forest for food. They eat fruit or other plant parts. Then they spread the plants' seeds through their droppings. How are the plants and animals helping each other?

15

PEOPLE OF THE FOREST

Humans have lived in the cloud forest for thousands of years. They use the forest for food and medicine. They also use materials from the forest to build their homes.

Today, some people who live in the forest are farmers. Others work for logging companies. Some are miners. They dig up minerals found in the ground.

Machu Picchu is a city built thousands of years ago. It is high in the South American cloud forest.

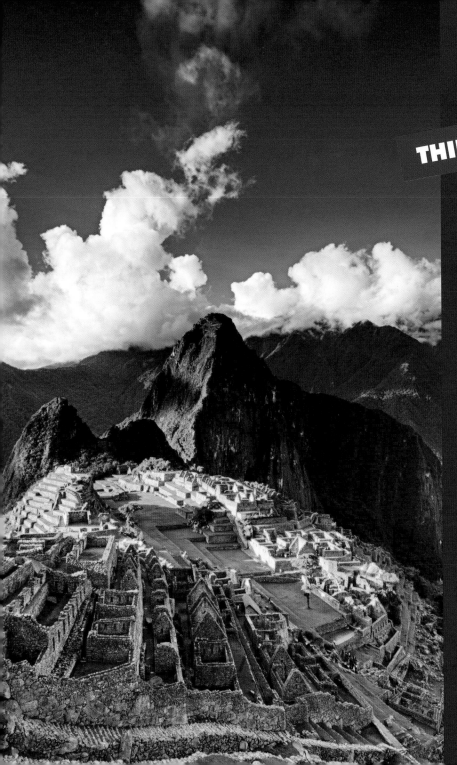

THINK!

Are humans hurting the cloud forest? Many scientists believe they are. Experts are especially worried when people cut down trees. This is called deforestation. Think about all the things that trees supply to the forest. Why is losing the trees a special problem?

19

The cloud forest is a unique and beautiful place. It offers many valuable resources. But it also must be protected. Many tourists and scientists travel to the area every year. They want to see this wonderful forest for themselves. Would you like to visit the cloud forest? What would you most like to see?

The South American cloud forest is a beautiful place!

Create a piece of art about South America's cloud forest. Perhaps it could tell a story! You could draw or paint a picture. You can also create a sculpture or diorama. You could even write a poem or song. Use your imagination!

GLOSSARY

biome (BYE-ohm) a type of area on Earth that is organized by which plants and animals live there

canopy (KAN-uh-pee) the upper level of a rain forest or cloud forest, consisting mostly of branches, vines, and leaves

diverse (di-VURS) having many different types or kinds

epiphytes (EP-uh-fytes) plants that don't need soil and get their nutrition from rain and the air

equator (i-KWAY-tur) an imaginary line around the middle of Earth that is equal distance from the North and South Poles

migrate (MYE-grate) to move to another area or climate at a specific time of year

nutrients (NOO-tree-uhnts) substances such as vitamins or minerals that living things need to stay healthy

omnivore (AHM-nuh-vor) an animal that eats both plants and animals

FIND OUT MORE

BOOK

Collard III, Sneed B. *The Forest in the Clouds*. Watertown, MA: Charlesbridge, 2000.

WEB SITES

Kids Discover—Discover Cloud Forests, Home to Horizontal Precipitation
www.kidsdiscover.com/quick-reads/discover-cloud-forests-home-horizontal-precipitation
Learn how plants get moisture right from the clouds!

Kona Cloud Forest Sanctuary—Kona Cloud Forest for Kids
www.konacloudforest.com/kona-cloud-forest-kids
This site lets kids share what they've learned about the cloud forest!

INDEX

ABOUT THE AUTHOR

Vicky Franchino loves to learn about new things—especially new places! The most interesting thing she learned about the cloud forest was that trees can "drink" and "eat" the clouds! Vicky had no idea clouds could be so important! She thinks it would be very interesting to visit the cloud forest. Vicky lives in Wisconsin with her family.

24